The Confident Canner

Answers to Your Canning Questions

Hestia's Hearth LLC

PO Box 7059

Kennewick, WA 99336

Email: info@SeedtoPantry.com

www.SeedtoPantry.com

ISBN: 978-0-9760137-8-5

Cover graphic: © Girlychic | Dreamstime.com

About the Author

Renee Pottle is the author of several cookbooks, a health educator specializing in Canning and Preserving and the owner of Hestia's Hearth LLC, a healthy eating company. Previously, she was a regular contributor to *Pillsbury Fast and Healthy Magazine* and for several years taught cooking, food science, nutrition, and health courses at a small school in Maine.

A frugal Yankee at heart, Renee first learned to can as a child while hanging out in her Nana's kitchen. She learned lots of family secrets while Nana and her sisters gossiped and put up jars and jars of pickles. But she also learned that growing and preserving food yourself saves money, keeps us connected to our family history, and tastes like Nana's love.

Renee and her husband make their home in Kennewick Washington where their sons, daughters-in-law and grandchildren visit often to raid the canning pantry!

Table of Contents

Introduction

Canning fresh fruits, vegetables, meats and fish is once again a popular past time. And why not? Canning allows us to re-experience the bright sunny days of summer when we need it most, during the long dark winter months. Opening a jar of brandied cherries or pickled asparagus in February reminds us that warm June days will come again. Canning takes our taste buds back to visions of lush Farmers' Markets and to sticky fingers, purple from pitting ripe Bing cherries.

But a lot has changed during the last quarter century. While most of us were quickly throwing together semi-made, highly processed meals from the grocery store freezer instead of preserving at home, home economists and other scientists continued to research the home preserving process. Along the way they discovered that many of Grandma's canning tips were no longer safe to follow. As it turns out, tomato puree needs to be processed in a water bath for much longer than we previously thought. Speaking of tomatoes, our newer hybrids are much less acidic than in years past, so we need to add lemon juice when canning them. Got an old family pickling recipe? It may not be safe either. Vinegar used to be sold at 7% acidity, today it's 5 percent.

Chances are if you are interested in canning at home you fall into one of two categories:

- Either you are a prolific gardener who needs to do something with all that produce from your back yard

- Or you are tired of not knowing exactly what is in your food and want a bit more control over your dinner plate

Canning is the perfect way to solve both problems. Canning isn't difficult. You don't need a college degree or to be a science whiz. But you do probably have questions. This book should answer all your questions, so you can confidently start canning today.

Happy canning!

General Canning

Just when you think you are ready to start today's canning project, a seemingly random question comes to mind. Perhaps you realize that you are missing a piece of canning equipment, or you suddenly have doubts about that old family jam recipe. This section seeks to put all those niggling little doubts to rest and ease your mind, so you can get that canning project started!

What a mess. One of my jars broke in the canner while processing. Why?

If you can long enough, it's only a matter of time until you end up with a broken jar. Sometimes the jar is brand new, and sometimes it is the oldest jar in your pantry, but the reason it breaks is usually the same; it has an unnoticed crack or chip. Jar cracks and chips can be microscopic, but when filled and placed in a water bath or pressure canner, the pressure causes the jar to break. Thoroughly check your jars before using and send damaged jars to the recycle bin.

Used mayonnaise or pickle jars may also break while processing. These jars are not made to be re-used and the glass is not as thick or strong as that of canning jars. Always use jars specifically designed for home canning.

Where should I store my home canned goods?

Home canned products should be stored in a cool, fairly dark place. Basement shelving or a closed pantry are perfect for storage. The most important thing is not to store canned good where they receive a lot of sunlight. Exposure to sunlight will cause home canned goods to rapidly degrade, reducing the quality of your products.

Do I really need to purchase all that canning equipment?

Although it may be easier to start canning with equipment

Hestia's Hearth LLC/Seed to Pantry
www.SeedtoPantry.com

specifically designed for home canning, you may be able to get by without purchasing anything. Any large pot can be turned into a water bath canner, as long as you have a rack or some other way to keep the jars off of the bottom of the pot.

A canning funnel is very helpful and will help reduce mess, but not absolutely necessary. Ditto for a bubble remover, you can use any long, non-metallic item like a serving spoon handle.

There are three things that you definitely need before home canning though; a jar lifter to lift hot jars out of boiling water, official canning jars and two piece lids (see question above), and if you are canning low-acid foods you will need a gauge-tested pressure canner.

Botulism is not commonly found in the soil in my area. So I don't have to worry about it when canning, right?

I usually hear this question from people who want to water bath their green beans instead of pressure canning. Sorry, home canning turns you into a food scientist, so it's best to think like a food scientist and not a cook. Just because botulism spores aren't common in your area doesn't mean that they aren't there. You wouldn't want to be the one who discovers them in your home canned products! Also, there are many other bacterias and molds that can cause serious illness from your home canned goods. It is best to always treat your home canning projects as if they have the potential to cause harm, and prepare and process following directions for the specific item.

Hestia's Hearth LLC/Seed to Pantry
www.SeedtoPantry.com

Do I still have to vent my self-venting canner?

This falls into the "better safe than sorry" category. Venting assures that all the air is removed from the canner. Air removal is necessary for the canner to reach the right temperature. Since self-venting canners don't actually always get rid of air, they must vented for 10 minutes before using.

My grandmother gave me her old dial-gauge pressure canner. Is it still safe to use?

Pressure canners tend to have a long life. Pressure canner gauges on the other hand may not work properly. It is always best to have your gauge tested before using - every year - no matter how old your canner is. Do note however, that canners made in the last 30 years are lighter and easier to use than older models.

Getting botulism from home canned goods is just an old wives' tale. Right?

So sorry. Every year there are stories of people who fall seriously ill or even die due to botulism poisoning. Several of these cases are from home canned goods, most often from improperly prepared and processed home canned fish, salsa, or other low-acid foods like green beans, asparagus, or corn.

Hestia's Hearth LLC/Seed to Pantry
www.SeedtoPantry.com

Which should I purchase, a dial gauge canner or a weighted gauge canner?

Both are perfectly fine and it usually comes down to personal preference. Dial gauges do need to be tested each year before use to assure that they are working correctly whereas weighted gauge canners do not need to be tested.

Weighted gauge canners will be noisier than dial gauge canners during processing, as the weighted gauge "knocks" while working.

I want to use all my old family canning recipes. They should still work fine, right?

It is not recommended that we use canning recipes that were created before 1994 unless they have been verified as safe.

Is it ok to design my own canning recipes?

The short answer is no. Changing a recipe by adding new ingredients or extra ingredients may make a perfectly safe recipe unsafe. For example, many people would like to add extra onions to an approved salsa recipe. However, since onions are a low-acid food, adding more onions than the recipe calls for would cause the recipe to become unsafe.

There are a few occasions when recipes can be changed. You can substitute sweet peppers for hot peppers in pickle recipes and vice versa. You can reduce or omit low-acid ingredients in

Hestia's Hearth LLC/Seed to Pantry
www.SeedtoPantry.com

pickles, for example you can leave the onions out entirely. You can substitute one berry for another in jam recipes. For example you can make blackberry jam using a blueberry jam recipe.

Does canning food make it less nutritious?

Somewhat. The most nutritious foods are those that are eaten immediately after being picked. Since most of us don't live this way, quickly frozen foods are usually the next most nutritious foods. Home canning does reduce the nutritive value of foods, but not to the extent that commercially canned foods do. Additionally, since home canned foods are put up in glass jars, there is no danger of BPA as there is in most commercially canned foods.

I keep hearing about open kettle canning. What is it?

Years ago canning procedures called for jars to be filled with hot ingredients and then turned on their tops to seal. Jars were not processed in a water bath canner. This process was especially used when making jams and is no longer considered safe. All jams should be processed in a water bath.

How do I know if the canning recipe I want to use is safe?

Recipes from reputable sources, published after 1994 should be safe. There have been some updates since that time though, for example pumpkin butter is no longer considered safe for water

Hestia's Hearth LLC/Seed to Pantry
www.SeedtoPantry.com

bath or home pressure canning.

Which foods are considered high acid?

High acid foods are those with a pH lower than 4.4. This includes vinegar, most fruits and some tomatoes. Foods that fall between 4.4 and 4.6 on the pH scale must be acidified before processing. These foods include most tomatoes and mangos. High acid foods can be processed using a water bath canner.

Which foods are considered low acid?

Low acid foods fall above 4.6 on the pH scale. These foods include meats, fish, vegetables, and some fruits like Asian pears and papaya. Low acid foods must be processed using a pressure canner.

I heard I should hot pack fruit. What is hot packing?

Fruits can usually be hot packed or cold packed. When hot packing, fruit is added to the hot syrup, heated through and then placed in the jars for processing. Cold packing has the fruit added to the jars, the hot syrup pored over it, and then processed. Hot packing does reduce the amount of fruit "float" but either process works fine.

Hestia's Hearth LLC/Seed to Pantry
www.SeedtoPantry.com

When do I need to adjust processing time for high elevation?

If you live over 1000 feet in elevation you will need to adjust processing time and/or pounds of pressure to assure safe processing. The usual adjustment is approximately 5 additional pounds of pressure or 5 additional minutes in a water bath for each additional altitude category. BUT, it is always a good idea to check with your county extension office for local recommendations as this general adjustment time may not result in a safe product.

Do I really have to sterilize jars before canning?

Nothing can turn a would-be home canner off of the process faster than the thought of having to have a big pot for canning and another big pot for sterilizing jars on the stove at the same time. Luckily canning jars do not have to be sterilized if they are to be processed for 10 minutes or longer. Recipes that call for a 5 minute processing time still have to be sterilized before using. Otherwise, jars should be clean and free of chips and cracks.

I do quite a bit of canning and am constantly going to the store to get more jar lids. Can't I just re-use them?

Disposable two-part jar lids cannot safely be reused (the rings of course are reusable). Plastic, reusable jar lids are now available, but are still a bit expensive.

My jars didn't seal during the water bath. What do I do now?

Often, jars that don't seal during the processing time will form a seal during the 12 hour cooling period. However, if this does not happen you can do one of two things. First, place the jar in the refrigerator and use that jar first. Secondly, re-process the jar in the water bath canner, once again for the entire processing time. If the jar does not seal this time, it should be refrigerated.

Is it ok to use honey instead of sugar?

Honey can be used to replace up to ½ of the amount of sugar in no-pectin added jams, or ¼ of the amount of sugar in pectin added jams. Honey can be used in place of sugar when making sweet pickles, but may lead to an unpalatable pickle.

My mother-in-law gave me boxes of empty mayonnaise jars to use for canning. Will these jars work ok?

No. Mayonnaise, pickle, and other commercial product jars are not designed to be used more than once and may break while being processed. Use jars designed for home canning for best results.

How should I label my home canned goods?

Home canned goods should be labeled with the product name,

date processed, source of recipe, processing method and time. Don't forget to add your name too! See example below.

Date: September 22, 2013 - Blue Ribbon Corn Relish
Recipe Source:
  Better Homes and Gardens Canning Publication, 2011
Ingredients: Fresh corn kernals, celery, bell peppers,
                onions, cider vinegar, sugar, dry mustard, salt,
                celery seeds. turmeric, cornstarch

Water Bath: 15 minutes

Pressure Canned:
                by Renee Pottle
                www.SeedToPantry.com

How long are my canned foods good? I have some that have been sitting on the shelf for years.

As long as home canned items are processed correctly and stay sealed, they will remain safe. However, the quality of home canned goods starts to degrade after one year. I recommend for best tasting products to consume them within one year. Pickles and jams remain tasty for 2 years.

I am new to canning. How do I tell if the jar has sealed?

A sealed jar lid will have no "give" to it when pushed down in the center with your finger. Often you can hear the jar seal when it is removed from the canner or as it cools as it will give off a popping sound. Jar lids that move up and down when pushed down in the center are not sealed and must either be reprocessed or refrigerated.

My jar is sealed, that means it is safe, right?

NO! A sealed jar is not necessarily a safe jar. The product inside may not have been processed correctly, a safe recipe may not have been used, or spoiled or molded ingredients may have been used, all of which will result in an unsafe product, even if the jar itself is sealed.

Last night I heard a sound in the pantry. Some of my jars were popping and there was salsa all over the place. I want to empty the jars into plastic containers and freeze the salsa. Ok?

NO! Popping jars is a sign of spoilage. The product may be infected with botulism or some other bacteria, yeast or mold. Using gloves, carefully empty popping jars into the garbage, close the bag and remove the garbage to another location. Rinse jars and run them through the dishwasher to sterilize. Never try to salvage product from popping jars. It can be frustrating to lose all your hard work, but you don't want to take the chance of illness.

Can I use a steam canner instead of my water bath canner?

Steam canners seem to be the perfect idea; they don't take up as much room, heat up much quicker than a water bath canner, and don't keep the kitchen so hot during the prime summer

canning season. But steam canners have not been verified as safe. Therefore, we don't know if the steam is actually able to penetrate the product in the jar. We don't know if it gets hot enough to kill all spoilage agents. And we don't actually know how long to process our products because there has not been any real testing. So turn your steam canner into a soup pot and keep using your water bath canner.

My friend told me not to use my glass top stove for canning. Is this true?

Most manufacturers don't recommend using a glass top stove for canning, but a very few seem to work. Apparently Frigidaire® brand usually works fine with most water bath canners (check your manufacturer's handbook before using). Also, try to purchase a canner with a flat bottom. I use my Frigidaire® cooktop to can with no problems. But I do believe that the burner I use (the largest) takes longer and longer to heat up each time I use it, meaning it is being adversely affected. And NEVER use a canner that is more than 1 inch wider in diameter than the glass cooktop burner, no matter what brand stove you own. It could cause the top to shatter.

My jars came out of the water bath covered in a white film. What happened?

First, relax. The white film does not mean that your product boiled out or that something is wrong. The film is most likely from hard water mineral deposits made during processing. To reduce this in the future, add up to one cup of vinegar to

Hestia's Hearth LLC/Seed to Pantry
www.SeedtoPantry.com

the boiling water bath water. Clean jars already covered with deposits with a disposable bleach cloth.

Can I use lime juice instead of lemon juice to acidify fruits and vegetables?

Yes, lime juice can be substituted for lemon juice in any home canning recipe. I especially like to add lime juice when making mango jam or green salsa. Just remember that lime has a distinctly different taste from lemon and will affect the taste of your product.

Why can't I process low acid foods in a water bath canner?

Two things combine to kill bacteria and other spoilage causing entities; acidity and heat. If a food is high acid, heating it to the boiling point for a specific length of time will kill off the bacteria. However, lower acid foods need heat that is higher than the boiling point of water. Since you cannot heat water higher than boiling on the stove, no matter how long you heat it, it must be placed under pressure to increase the temperature to the point where it will kill off the bacteria. That can only be done using some sort of pressure canner.

Hestia's Hearth LLC/Seed to Pantry
www.SeedtoPantry.com

What's the difference between a pressure canner and a pressure cooker?

Pressure canners and pressure cookers work under the same premise, but a pressure cooker is too small to can items. Most pressure cookers are 4 or 8 quarts, while a pressure canner is usually a 17 quart pot.

I have been canning for a while now and find that I am losing track of all my canning projects. How do I keep them organized?

There are many reasons why it makes good sense to write down your projects, but the most important reason for me is to keep track so I don't waste food!

The time to start a journal isn't months after you've starting canning (sadly this is from my very own experience), the time is now – while we are getting ready for a new canning and preserving season. But, while a canning journal is a very practical and time saving object, it also can be a creative endeavor much like scrap booking, card making, or….. canning!

Those of you who love the kitchen but are all thumbs with paper, glue, and crafts may choose to purchase a canning journal to keep your projects organized. I have included some resources in the back.

But if you are ready to design your own journal, be sure to include the following:

1. Start with a simple paper or online graph. My canning journal is designed so the paper is landscape, but you can also orient the paper in a portrait direction.

2. Include a space for each:

- Date – at least the month and year

- Product – what you are preserving, for example Strawberry Jam

- Amount – how many containers you preserved

- Size – what was the size of those containers, for example quart jars or gallon freezer bags

- Ingredients – what ingredients were used. This is a good place to write down specific types of fruits/veggies. For example, that you made that yummy apple butter with Cortland and Golden Delicious apples.

- Technique – how was the item processed; was it water bathed? frozen? pressure canned?

- Time – how long did the processing take? Did you process the tomato puree for 40 minutes in a water bath?

3. Add extra pages or spaces for Notes and Recipes. You may want to include a space for notes on each line. Or, you may prefer to add several pages for your own handwritten notes and favorite recipes in the back of the journal.

Hestia's Hearth LLC/Seed to Pantry
www.SeedtoPantry.com

4. Make several copies of each blank page, enough to last you a year or more. Don't forget to make the copies double-sided.

5. Choose a front and back cover. This is a good place to show off those decoupage or drawing skills. Make sure your name is displayed prominently on the cover as your canning journal will soon become a family heirloom! Use cover stock weight paper or get your covers laminated at a local print shop.

6. Either 3 hole punch the pages and enclose in a notebook, or have your local print shop bind the journal. Or, if you are interested in making your own books, research unusual bookbinding techniques.

I have a terrible time finding gifts for my mother-in-law, but she is a prolific home canner. Do you have any good gift ideas?

Anyone on your list would be happy to receive one of these home canning gifts, whether they are new to canning or have been canning for decades.

Fancy Canning Jars: Home canners are always looking for something a little different. Most fancy canning jars come from Europe, and the price reflects the boat trip. I love the little **tulip jars by Weck**. They are perfect for sharing lemon or orange curd with loved ones.

And **Bormioli Rocco Stagioni jars** would be perfect filled with rose petal or elderberry jam.

Diamond shaped **Leifhiet** jars would be perfect for pickled peppers or homemade giardiniera.

If you are purchasing jars for someone else, don't feel that you have to fill them with something first. To you, a box of empty jars may seem like a strange gift, but we canners know and appreciate unusual and hard-to-find jars. Don't worry – we'll fill them ourselves next summer.

Electric Water Bath Canner: Here is something for someone you really love. Today's glass top stoves are not recommended for canning. The heat gets trapped under the canner and can lead to a shattered glass ranged top. Usually I recommend using a three – legged propane camp stove and canning outside, but that isn't the answer for everyone. An **electric water bath canner** is the answer. It works just like a good, old-fashioned canner, only you set it on the counter instead of the stove top and plug it in. Someday I am going to own one of these.

Food Dehydrator: **Food dehydrators** come in all shapes and sizes. There are small inexpensive versions and large commercial grade versions. Unless your gift recipient dries tons of fruit or vegetables, a smaller dehydrator will be perfect. Really, all brands work well. Just be sure that the dehydrator has a thermometer attached.

So Easy to Preserve: This **book**, written by the experts at the University of Georgia, answers almost every question you could ever ask about canning, dehydrating, and freezing food. There are hundreds of recipes, charts, and suggestions

Hestia's Hearth LLC/Seed to Pantry
www.SeedtoPantry.com

Other Canning Books: Newer canning books like **Saving the Season** by Kevin West are always welcome. And don't forget that your recipient might enjoy a copy of **The Confident Canner**. Some canners enjoy old canning books and booklets that can be found at yard sales on used book stores, especially those from the heyday of canning, the 1930's and 1940's.

Where exactly will I find safe canning recipes?

Master Food Preservers/County Extension Offices: The Master Food Preserver program is offered through many county extension offices nationwide. Master Food Preservers are trained to educate about food safety, home canning and preserving. Master Food Preservers can help you find safe recipes for anything you want to preserve – provided it can be safely preserved at home. If a product can't be safely preserved at home, like canned sun-dried tomatoes in oil, they will let you know that too!

Home Economists/Family and Consumer Scientists: Home Economists are another good source for food safety in general and home canning in particular. While not every Home Economist specializes in foods, every Home Economist does know when to question a safe food product.

National Center for Home Food Preservation : The national center, housed at the University of Georgia, is a nationwide clearing house for all things home canning and preserving.

Here you will find tutorials, recipes, articles, information, and more – all devoted to safe home food preservation.

Larger Companies (Ball/Kerr, Better Homes and Gardens, Heinz): Anyone can put up a site and post canning recipes. The problem is, we often don't know if those recipes have been tested for safety or not. But, we can probably be pretty sure that large companies such as those above who sell canning supplies, magazines, and booklets have fully tested every recipe before it is published. So you can be satisfied that recipes are safe. Just check the copyright date on older print material. Recipes published before 1994 may not be considered safe. Find a more recent version of the recipe by checking out the company website.

Cookbooks by Qualified Authors: There are lots of new canning cookbooks out there. Some are wonderfully creative. Others are questionably creative. How do you tell the difference? Learn about the author. Is the author a Master Food Preserver or a Home Economist? If so, the recipes most likely have been tested for safety. If not, check the publisher. Is the publisher a large company? If so, they most likely have had the recipes tested for safety. If the author doesn't seem to have any "official" qualifications, and the book is self-published or published by a smaller company, the recipes may still all be safe. Or they may not be. It's hard to tell. My advice would be to pass on the book, or email the publisher/author asking if the recipes are verified safe for home canning.

Naturally I can't guarantee that every recipes found from

Hestia's Hearth LLC/Seed to Pantry
www.SeedtoPantry.com

the above sources will be perfectly safe. There are too many variables for that. But I can guarantee that you are much more likely to find a safe home canning recipe from the above sources than you would just surfing the net.

Hestia's Hearth LLC/Seed to Pantry
www.SeedtoPantry.com

Jams and Jellies

Jams, jellies, and other soft spreads like fruit butters, preserves, and marmalades can be a sweet introduction to home canning. After all, there's nothing quite like opening a jar of fragrant apricot or blackberry jam in the dead of winter, to remind us that summer will indeed come once again. Soft spreads also offer enough variety to assure that everyone on your gift list will find something they like; whether apple-cinnamon butter, tangy orange marmalade, or rich raspberry jam.

Do I have to add powdered or liquid pectin to homemade jam?

There are many jam recipes that do not call for added pectin, although adding pectin does make a quicker jam. Jam made with added pectin requires more sugar than long-cooking jams. Also, some people are sensitive to gums and pectins and pectin-added jams cause stomach upsets. Jellies on the other hand almost always require added pectin, unless you are making a naturally high-pectin jelly like apple or grape.

What is pectin?

Pectin is the naturally occurring gum that allows a jam or jelly to set up (in conjunction with acid). Some fruits, like apples, Concord grape and citrus, are naturally high in pectin. Others, like peaches and most berries, have almost no natural pectin.

What is a fruit conserve?

Fruit conserves are similar to jams, but usually include nuts and sometimes raisins. Fruit conserves can be eaten as jams spread on bread, or as a sweet condiment, much like many relishes.

Can I substitute liquid pectin for powdered pectin when making jam?

No. Recipes written for liquid pectin usually do not work well with powdered pectin and vice versa.

Is it ok to use sugar substitutes like Splenda® or Equal® when making jam?

If you are using a sugar substitute you must use a low-sugar pectin product designed specifically for sugar substitutes. Long cooking jams also do not work well with sugar substitutes as the substitute becomes bitter with the cooking time. Many people have better luck making freezer jam if they want to use a sugar substitute.

I love jelly, but juicing fruit takes too long. Is it ok to use canned juice from the grocery store?

Purchased juice can be used if it is unpasteurized juice. Most commercially prepared juice has been processed and the pectin removed, therefore jelly made with it won't set.

Why are there crystals in my grape jelly?

Sometimes crystals form in grape jelly from a naturally occurring acid found in grapes. Growing conditions affect the amount of this acid, so you may not be able to completely eliminate them. Reduce the chance by straining the grape juice

and letting it sit in the refrigerator for up to 5 days before making jelly.

What is clear gel?

Instant Clear Jel is a form of corn starch that does not need to be heated in order to set. It can be used to make low sugar jams, but should be combined with the sugar first to avoid lumpy jam.

What is Pamona's Universal Pectin®?

Unlike Clear Jel, Pamona's Universal Pectin® is a special kind of pectin product that allows you to make jams and jellies with low or no sugar. The pectin uses a calcium phosphate powder to help set up, thus allowing for less sugar.

Help! My homemade jam is moldy on the top. Can I just scrape the mod off and eat the rest of the jam?

Moldy food should be thrown out. Although it may look like the mold is just on the top, that is seldom true. Microscopic mold, which will still make people sick, probably has penetrated well into the jar.

Is there a way make jelly without added pectin?

Only a few fruits contain enough natural pectin and acid to make a good jelly without added pectin. Those most likely to have a good result are apples, crabapples, grapes, some plums and tart cherries.

My long cooking jams never seem to set up. Why?

Long cooking jams can be difficult to get just right. Think of long cooking jams as a science experiment. Outside forces can affect the success or failure of the jam. For example, if you are trying to cook a batch of long cooking jam on a steamy, humid day the batch will probably never set up. Why? Because the air is so full of water that the sugar/fruit combination cannot keep up with it.

Another reason could be impatience. Long cooking jams can take a nearly an hour to reach the jelling point. That is a long time to stir and tend to a pot of bubbling fruit. To assure success, make sure that you have the correct amount of fruit, sugar and acid by following an approved recipe, and cook the combination to the gelling point.

My cooking jam is making a mess! How do I keep it from boiling over?

This is my all-time favorite tip. Before you start cooking the fruit/sugar mixture, rub butter or margarine around the top of the saucepot. The fat keeps the jam from boiling over.

Hestia's Hearth LLC/Seed to Pantry
www.SeedtoPantry.com

Is there any way to decrease the amount of foam that forms on the cooking jam?

Stirring constantly will keep the foam down. But that can be a lot of stirring! Adding a teaspoon or so of butter to the cooking jam will also decrease the foam. Once you have removed the jam from the heat, but before adding it to the canning jars, you can stir vigorously and usually stir the foam down. If all else fail, skim the foam off the top before putting the jam in the jars.

My Mom always used paraffin wax to top her jam, and didn't process the jars in a water bath. Can I just follow her directions?

I remember my mother making jam the same way, but the paraffin wax approach is no longer considered safe. Processing jam in a water bath adds an extra measure of safety and helps the jam stay good for a longer period of time. (I also remember opening a new jar of jam, removing the paraffin only to find a layer of mold- yuck!) Using the water bath method is less messy than playing around with potentially flammable paraffin too.

Even though I use butter around the top of my saucepot, the cooking jam still spits and gets all over the kitchen. Is there any way to prevent this from happening?

I have a habit of falling into this trap too because my favorite saucepot is really too small for a regular batch of jam. Using a

larger saucepot/Dutch oven will reduce and even eliminate the "sticky kitchen syndrome."

I love to make jam, but most recipes just call for too much sugar. Can I reduce the sugar amount?

Yes and no. Long cooking, no-pectin added recipes must be made with the prescribed amount of sugar. Sugar helps the jam set up, and also acts as a preservative in these recipes. Reducing the sugar amount would result in either a runny jam and/or a jam that cannot be safely stored at room temperature.

Some jams that use added pectin can be made with less sugar. Be sure to purchase the "low-sugar" specific pectin and follow the insert directions. Freezer jams can also be made with less sugar as they are preserved in the freezer.

Can I use honey or maple syrup in jam?

You can replace up to half of the sugar with an equal amount of honey or maple syrup, and cook as you would normally. Honey and maple syrup will change the flavor of your jam though, as they both have quite a bit of flavor on their own. I personally like to use maple syrup with apple spreads or anything cranberry. Honey adds a mellowness to peach that I just love.

This summer is just too hot to make jam! Can I freeze the fresh fruit and then make it into jam this fall?

Absolutely. This is a great idea, especially if you live in one of this summer's "hot zones." Peaches, all berries, and cherries freeze especially well. When you are ready to turn them into jam just measure out the correct amount (don't even have to thaw) and proceed with the recipe.

Why do some jam recipes call for the addition of lemon juice and some do not?

Lemon juice is added to some fruits to increase the acid content. This is especially important if you are making long cooking jams that do not call for added pectin. A high acid level helps the jam set, or gel. Fruit that naturally has a lower acid level (like peaches) usually needs lemon juice added. Lime juice may be added instead if you like. Lemon juice is also sometimes added to help keep the fruit from turning brown.

I want to make large amounts of jam to give as Christmas presents, but I don't want to spend all day cooking. Can't I just double or triple the jam recipe?

Sorry, the answer is no. Jams work best when made in small batches. Large batches of jam made at home (without commercial equipment designed for large batches) often result in burned, over-cooked jam. Stick to small batches for perfect jams and other soft spreads

How can I tell when long cooking jams or preserves are set? I always seem to overcook them.

This is a common problem, especially if you are new to long cooking no pectin added jams. There are a couple of ways to check. My favorite is to drop some of the cooking jam onto a glass plate and put it in the fridge for a minute. If the jam sets up to the level you like (there is no such thing as the "right" level, only the level you prefer) remove the cooking jam from the heat and ladle it into the jars. Another way is to drop some of the cooking jam onto a glass plate that is already cold. Draw a spoon through the jam. If the line stays separated, the jam is done. You can also check by temperature. Jam is usually set when the temperature reaches 8-9 degrees above the temperature of boiling water. Water usually boils at 212 degrees, but not always. Several things can affect the temperature including altitude and barometric pressure. So if you choose to use this method, check today's boiling water temperature first, otherwise you may end up with burnt jam from cooking too long.

My batch of jam didn't set. Is there any way to salvage it?

There are a variety of reasons why long cooking jams and preserves might not set. Since we don't add pectin, the fruit acidity is very important. Some fruits are just not acid enough to ever set without pectin added (melons for example). But sometimes the fruit is just too ripe so the acid level is a little low. Sometimes the jam wasn't cooked long enough to set. Cooking time fluctuates with the weather, so even if your raspberry

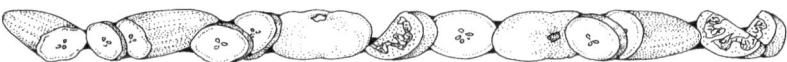

Hestia's Hearth LLC/Seed to Pantry
www.SeedtoPantry.com

jam last week cooked in 30 minutes, this week it may take 40 minutes or even 20 minutes. So here's what to do:

• Spoon all the undercooked jam into a large saucepot.

• Add about 1 tsp lemon juice for each cup of jam.

• Bring to a boil and cook until jam sets.

• Remove from heat and pour into clean jars.

Seal and process in a water bath canner for 10 – 15 minutes.

Oh no! My homemade jam is thick and almost like candy! How can I fix it?

It's is harder to salvage overcooked jam. If the jam tastes scorched it's best just to throw it away and try again. If the jam isn't scorched but is too thick to use as jam, slowly heat it in the microwave with a little added water and use it as syrup. I also have used overcooked jam in place of honey in homemade BBQ sauce, stir-fry sauce, or in the center of muffins. You could also melt overcooked jam in the microwave and brush it over pound cake or bar cookies.

Hestia's Hearth LLC/Seed to Pantry
www.SeedtoPantry.com

Pickles

Nothing perks up a boring meal like a pickle. It almost seems too easy, simply combining cucumbers, carrots or green beans with vinegar, sprinkled with a little bit of magic, and we have an appetizer, a meal extender, or a sandwich enhancer. Pickles are spicy or sweet, tangy or tart, crunchy or smooth. And there is no better way to save cucumber or zucchini garden overload than to turn them into jars of beautiful pickles.

Can I make pickles from cucumbers purchased at the grocery store?

Yes, but beware of two things. First, most grocery store cucumbers have been waxed and you will need to scrub the wax off before using. Secondly, purchase the thinnest grocery store cucumbers you can find. Most pickle recipes call for pickling cukes which are smaller than traditional grocery store cukes. You will get best results with thinner cucumbers.

What is pickling salt?

Pickling salt is basically regular everyday salt that has no additives. Most table salt includes additives to make it flow smoothly. These additives can cause home canned pickles to be cloudy. Kosher salt may be used instead of pickling salt.

Can I pressure can my pickles?

Yes, although it may result in soft pickles. The water bath method works better for pickles.

Why is my homemade sauerkraut pink?

That pink color is a sign of yeast growth. Yeast growth is usually caused by using too much salt or by the salt not being evenly mixed with the shredded cabbage. Pink sauerkraut

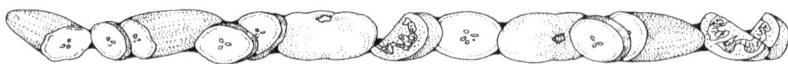

Hestia's Hearth LLC/Seed to Pantry
www.SeedtoPantry.com

should be thrown away and not eaten.

My pickles look great. How long do they have to sit before I can eat them?

Although you can open a jar of pickles as soon as they coo from the canner, for best flavor wait at least three weeks before opening.

I am on a low salt diet. Is it ok to reduce the amount of salt in my pickle recipe?

The amount of salt in fermented pickles cannot be reduced, as the salt keeps the fermenting pickles from spoiling. Fresh pack pickles, those made with vinegar, do not need salt for a safe product.

I heard that I should use low temperature processing for my pickles. What is low temperature processing?

There is always a balance between making a crisp pickle and making a safe pickle. Low temperature processing allows both to happen.

1. Heat water in a canner to 120 degrees Fahrenheit

2. Add filled jars and enough water to cover the jars.

3. Heat the water to 180 degrees Fahrenheit, but keep the temperature below 185 degrees Fahrenheit.

4. Process for 30 minutes.

5. Remove jars from canner and let cool.

This method is only for recipes that are designed for low-temperature processing.

Can I use sugar substitutes like Splenda® or Equal® in sweet pickles?

No, sugar substitutes become bitter when processed with vinegar.

Why is my pickled asparagus (or green beans, or okra, etc.) slimy?

Slimy pickled goods indicate bacteria or some other infecting agent. The pickled goods should be thrown away.

Why is my pickled asparagus wrinkled?

Pickled asparagus and pickled green beans often become wrinkled from the vinegar pushing water out of the cell walls.

Hestia's Hearth LLC/Seed to Pantry
www.SeedtoPantry.com

This does not affect quality. Often the wrinkling will go away as the jars of pickles sit.

I don't have a stone crock for fermented pickles. Can I make them in a new garbage can?

No. Garbage cans are treated with disinfectants, even new ones. Use a food grade plastic or glass crock to ferment pickles. Restaurants may have large empty food grade containers from pickles or sauces that they would be willing to sell or give away.

How do I keep my pickles crisp?

There are a variety of ways to keep your pickles crisp.

*   Low temperature processing.

*   Soak raw cucumbers in ice water and salt before processing.

*   Add clean oak or grape leaves to each jar of pickles. The tannins in the leaves do add a bitter flavor, but some old-time recipes call for them.

*   Use Pickle Crisp® – a calcium chloride product that keeps the pickles crisp. Follow directions on the jar. Pickle Crisp® can be found with the canning supplies.

Hestia's Hearth LLC/Seed to Pantry
www.SeedtoPantry.com

What kind of vinegar is best for pickling?

You can use any kind of vinegar as long as it is 5% acidity. White vinegar lends a sharp vinegary taste. Apple cider vinegar is more mellow, but colors the pickles somewhat. Red wine vinegar, balsamic vinegar, champagne vinegar, etc all add their own unique flavor to pickles, but are quite expensive to use when making large numbers of pickles. Vinegar can be used interchangeably as long as it is 5%. So if a recipe calls for white vinegar, you can use apple cider vinegar or red wine vinegar instead – just as long as it is 5 percent.

Why can't I use my aluminum pots when making pickles?

Aluminum, copper, brass, and iron all interact with vinegar and will lead to a metallic tasting pickle. Use stainless steel, enamelware, or glass pots for best results.

What kinds of cucumbers are best for pickling?

You will get the best results when using pickling cucumber varieties. Pickles made from small or immature slicing cucumbers will not be as high quality.

Tomatoes and Other Fruits

Tomatoes and their fruit cousins can easily be canned for use all year long. This is one area where you can really save money when canning, especially if your family enjoys many tomato based products like marinara sauce, homemade soups, and barbeque sauce. Plus, when canning your own tomatoes and fruits, you won't have to worry about potentially harmful BPA exposure or excessively sugary fruit.

How do I pasteurize my homemade cider?

Yummmm – homemade cider is a delicious treat. But, it is always a good idea to pasteurize it before sampling. Simply heat the cider to 160 degrees Fahrenheit. Store cider in the refrigerator or keep in the freezer.

Do I have to pasteurize homemade cider?

Since homemade cider can easily be infected with bacteria, it is always a good idea to pasteurize it. The bacteria may come from a variety of places; not using clean containers to store the cider, using a cider press that hasn't been cleaned, or most common – from apples that have fallen to the ground and been infected by deer or other animal manure.

Help! My canned fruit has floated to the top of the jar. How do I prevent this from happening again?

Floating fruit is usually the result of one of two things. Either the jar is not full of fruit or it was cold packed. To reduce floating fruit be sure to hot pack your fruit. Floating fruit, while not as attractive in the jar as non-floating fruit, still tastes great!

How do I acidify tomatoes before canning?

Add 1 Tbsp of lemon juice per pint jar of tomatoes or 2 Tbsp per quart jar.

Everyone loves my secret recipe spaghetti sauce. Is it ok to can some of it this year?

I understand that you may want to can your own spaghetti sauce recipe, but it is not a good idea since your secret sauce has not been checked for canning safely. However, all is not lost. You can do one of three things; make your secret sauce while the tomatoes are ripe and freeze it; follow a similar approved canning recipe and then add your secret ingredients at mealtime; or can pureed tomato sauce and turn it into your sauce as you open the cans.

Yuck! I don't like jalapeno peppers. Can I use other peppers in my salsa recipe?

This is one of the few changes that you can safely make to a canning recipe. Instead of jalapenos you can use bell peppers, other hot peppers, or leave the peppers out entirely. Just be sure to use the measurement the recipe calls for, no more.

How long should I process canned tomatoes?

Tomato processing times have increased over the last few years. Don't forget to acidify your tomatoes and process in a water

bath canner for the following times at 0-1000 ft. elevation:

- Crushed/Pureed: Pints for 35 minutes, Quarts for 45 minutes

- Whole tomatoes in water: Pints for 40 minutes, Quarts for 45 minutes

- Whole Tomatoes in Juice: Pints for 85 minutes, Quarts for 85 minutes

- Whole Tomatoes w/out Added Liquid: Pints and Quarts for 85 minutes

I love stewed tomatoes but don't own a pressure canner. Can I process them in a water bath?

Sadly no. Because stewed tomatoes include low-acid ingredients like peppers and onion, they must be processed in a pressure canner to assure safety. If you don't want to purchase a pressure canner, you could freeze your stewed tomatoes.

Do I have to peel tomatoes before canning? It just seems like so much work!

No, tomatoes do not have to be peeled before canning. Most people peel them as a personal choice.

Why do I have to acidify tomatoes? I don't remember my mother ever doing so.

Today's tomatoes are less acidic than those in the past. Therefore, tomatoes need to be acidified before canning.

Why did my canned pears turn pink?

This is a natural occurrence that is related to the growing conditions. As long as the pears were prepared and processed correctly they are safe to eat.

Do I have to add sugar when canning fruit?

No, fruit can be canned in water, apple juice or sugar syrup. Fruit canned without sugar though, will not remain high quality as long as fruit canned with at least some sugar, and should be eaten within a few months.

Why did my home canned tomato juice separate?

Home canners and commercial canners use different methods to separate tomato juice from its pulp. Because the commercial method is so much quicker that what we can do at home, pectin does not bread down during the extraction process. Therefore, the pectin continues to hold the tomato cells in suspension. In other words, the commercial method gets the juice before the cells know what hit them! Home juice extraction is a slower

process, causing the pectin to break down and the juice to separate.

Why did last year's canned peaches turn brown on the top?

This can, and will eventually happen to all canned fruit. The brown color is a result of oxidation, as the air trapped in the top of the jar comes in contact with the fruit. Although it does not affect safety (unless the jar has lost its seal), it does adversely affect fruit quality. Fruit that has been around long enough so that it turns brown on the top should probably be tossed, as it will no longer have a good flavor.

Some of the liquid in my tomatoes boiled out during the water bath. Why?

Most likely the water bath was boiling too high. Tomatoes have a long processing time, and a highly boiling water bath pushes the liquid out of the jar.

Is it ok to can over-ripe tomatoes?

Over-ripe tomatoes do not result in a good quality canned product. However, since we don't want to waste our beautiful, but over-ripe fruits:

Hestia's Hearth LLC/Seed to Pantry
www.SeedtoPantry.com

Combine the over-ripe tomatoes with some slightly under-ripe tomatoes and make canned puree.

Make your own sauce from the over-ripe tomatoes and freeze it for future use.

I like to make salsa with tomatillos but can't find a recipe. What should I do?

The National Center for Home Food Preservation site has a tomatillo salsa recipe that is very good. Also, any salsa recipe that calls for green tomatoes can be used interchangeably with tomatillos.

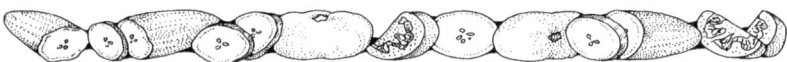

50

Canning Vegetables, Meat, and Fish

Low acid foods like meats, broths, fish and seafood and vegetables require special considerations when canning at home. Because these foods lack a high acid content, they must be canned with a pressure canner to assure that they are safe to eat. Many people are scared off from old-time stories of pressure canners exploding on the stove or jars not properly sealing and opt to freeze low-acid foods instead. But if you love canned green beans, or chicken, or home canned tuna, go ahead and can it! Today's pressure canners are safe, reliable, and easy to use as long as you follow the directions. Just be sure to follow an approved canning recipe.

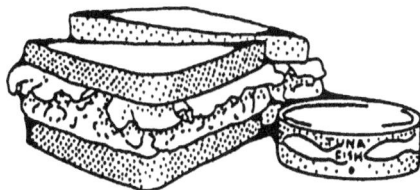

Is it ok to can fish in quart jars?

No, fish and seafood should be canned in pint or half-pint jars only. No safe processing times for quart jars has been identified.

We have a bumper crop of pumpkins this year. How do I can pumpkin puree or pumpkin butter?

It has been determined that because there is no way to standardize the thickness of home canned pumpkin puree and butter, no safe processing method has been determined. Therefore homemade pumpkin butter and/or puree should be frozen for long-term storage. Pumpkin or winter squash cubes may be canned following a low-acid method.

I want to can homemade pesto for later. Where will I find a recipe?

Pesto, much like pumpkin puree, is very difficult to standardize. The best way to save homemade pesto is to freeze it. No safe method of home canning has been identified for pesto.

Hestia's Hearth LLC/Seed to Pantry
www.SeedtoPantry.com

I saw this great idea to can banana bread. Is it safe to do so?

A few years ago it *seemed* like a good idea to bake quick breads in a canning jar, cover them and let them sit on the shelf. However, quick breads are a wonderful breeding ground for bacteria and molds; they are low acid, moist, warm, and when sealed in a jar become the perfect environment for botulism to grow. Quick breads baked in canning jars is a cute way to bake them, but they should never be sealed and should be eaten right away.

Is it ok to water bath green beans?

Green beans and other vegetables are low-acid and as such must be processed in a pressure canner to prevent infection.

Why can't I just process low-acid foods in a water bath for a longer period?

It takes a combination of factors to kill off bacteria, usually acid plus heat. That is why high acid foods like most fruits and pickles are safely processed in a water bath. The boiling water plus the high acid content of the foods themselves will kill the bacteria.

When we don't have a high acid environment though, it takes more than just boiling water to kill bacteria. A water bath temperature will never get higher than the boiling point, no

matter how long we let it boil. The only way to increase the water temperature is to put it under pressure. That is why we use a pressure canner. The pressure allows the water temperature to climb higher than the boiling point, or high enough to kill the bacteria in low-acid foods. ALWAYS follow approved canning directions and temperatures. Processing low-acid foods in a water bath is potentially deadly.

Do I have to add salt to my canned vegetables?

No, salt is added for flavor only and may safely be left out of canned vegetables.

Hestia's Hearth LLC/Seed to Pantry
www.SeedtoPantry.com

Canning Resources

Blogs

Seed to Pantry - Your home for everything about canning, preserving, cooking from the garden and urban homesteading kitchen projects. Look for it here first!

A Gardener's Table – Linda Ziedrich's wonderful blog about all things to grow and preserve.

Food in Jars – Marisa McClellan writes this popular canning blog, full of recipes, class schedules, and giveaways.

Real Food – While not strictly a canning blog, this blog from Mother Earth News has everything you'll ever want to know about canning, and homesteading.

Saving the Season – Kevin West is the author of this fantastic blog and book of the same name.

Canning Aids

Canning and Preserving Journal – Designed and personalized especially for you. Find both print and downloadable pdf versions on the Seed to Pantry website.

How to Can App – free from Mother Earth News.

Canning Jars - Weck, Bormioli Rocco, Leifheit and Ball/Kerr jars can all be found on the Amazon.com website.

Electric Water Bath Canner - Ball has recently come out with a reasonable priced electric water bath canner and multi-cooker. You can find it on their website at FreshPreserving.com.

Food Dehydrator - Inexpensive food dehydrators can be found at almost any department store. All work well. Food dehydrators should have a thermometer attached for safe drying.

So Easy to Preserve - This book can be purchased at your local county extension office, on the Amazon.com website, or from the National Center for Home Food Preservation at nchfp.uga. edu/publications.

Hestia's Hearth LLC/Seed to Pantry
www.SeedtoPantry.com

www.ingramcontent.com/pod-product-compliance
Lightning Source LLC
Chambersburg PA
CBHW071738020426
42331CB00008B/2078